> TABLE OF CONTENTS <

D1524023

INTRODUCTION

Hello and welcome! As a fellow traveler, you have many options around how you choose to spend your valuable time, so I'd like to give you my thanks for taking the time to check out this book!

Now before getting into the main content about exploring the amazing Mayan city of Chichen Itza — I'd like to share a bit about myself and what inspired me to write this travel guide.

My name is Andreu Limongi — I grew up in the United States, in South Florida; my childhood was filled with the typical things a kid of the 80's had growing up: Disney, Looney Tunes, Legos, Transformers, and Nintendo games. Of course, I still love these things today. Now you might already be asking yourself what any of this has to do with the Mayan culture, archaeology, or the city of Chichen Itza..

This may sound unusual, but my curiosity and interest in Mayan culture was sparked long ago by an obscure Nintendo video game named "Tombs and Treasure".

This was a game released back in 1991 on the original 8-bit Nintendo console. My brother and I rented it from a local video rental store one weekend. We took turns, argued, and had to actually *work together* to figure out all its secrets.

Tombs and Treasure is a graphical adventure set in the ruins of an ancient city Mayan named Chichen Itza, with the goal being to find a missing archaeologist while defeating various Mayan demons and solving all sorts of interesting and challenging puzzles.

The game was quite fun (I finished it several times) but what always stuck with me was how it was based on a real-life place. It did a good job of introducing its audience to Chichen Itza, and it featured a cool story (for a game at least) based on a real-world location.

In 2018 (about thirty years later) I took my first trip to the Yucatán peninsula and was able to visit Chichen Itza for the first time, and I was absolutely blown away by the experience. What I had found so interesting and cool as a kid (that I understood was a real place) had finally manifested into my reality — like stepping back into my childhood, getting to *live* that old video game. I admit this is very nerdy, but it's 100% true. I'm not ashamed about it at all :)

On this first trip to Chichen Itza, I arrived at around 1-2pm local time and was stuck with a tour group that had scheduled around 3 hours total at the site, with two of those hours on a slow-paced guided tour of the city. I was left with only 60 minutes at the end to explore and check out what I wanted, how I wanted.

To me, this was absolutely criminal.. and I had no idea if I would have another chance to come back, and see the ruins my way.

Two days later, I booked an early morning tour which arrived at 8:00am, right when the site opens for visitors. This time around, I saw everything I wanted to see, at my own pace, on my own schedule — and for me it was infinitely better and far more rewarding.

This approach is what I recommend to anyone considering a visit to Chichen Itza, and what I hope to help you do with this guide.

Sounds fun, right? Then let's get started!

The Red House (Casa Colorada) at Chichen Itza

TIPS ON USING THIS GUIDE

Something to keep in mind is that this book is not designed to be a comprehensive or full-length historical guide to everything you could possibly want to know about the Mayan cities on the Yucatán. There are many books already available for that purpose.

My goal is to share some ideas and options to consider, which may help make your trip more memorable and fulfilling. Therefore you can expect to see just a little bit of history and culture notes throughout the various sections of this book, but hopefully not too much to distract you from experiencing the ruins in the flesh.

To put it another way — there are people who go to concerts and choose to hold up their phone to record the performance, but they are not fully 100% present in the music or in the moment.

I feel that the same concept applies when exploring new, amazing places that you might not experience again in the future. This is of course, a very individual and personal decision, but the content in this guide will lean towards encouraging you to be fully present in the ancient energy of Chichen Itza, and to explore the environment with your senses. This guide will lightly sprinkle in some historical context as needed, but no long academic discussion. Our goal is to see and experience the Mayan ruins in person; you'll have plenty of time to read and educate yourself on the way home.

In addition, we'll be covering a lot of ideas around logistics and planning various aspects of your trip, i.e. how to make sure that your travel experience is as smooth and stress-free as possible.

At the end of this guide there will also be a reference section with links to additional resources on the web, which can supplement the topics and suggestions from this book with more detail.

To summarize, please think of this book as a quick reference guide, with a bit of facts and history to pique your interest in learning and exploring more on your own. There are many additional resources at your fingertips if you're interested in diving deeper into any aspect of Mayan history, civilization, or Mexico in general.

Now then, let's learn a bit more about the Mayan civilization!

* * *

A BRIEF HISTORY OF THE MAYA

Throughout the course of recorded time, there have been dozens (if not hundreds) of incredible civilizations that have each contributed something special to the world. The Maya have certainly made their mark here as well, and their history as a people has many interesting aspects — in almost any given category of human achievement, the Maya demonstrate near-unmatched craftsmanship, striking intellect, notable precision, and a powerful intensity.

The Maya flourished in the Yucatán peninsula from around 600 - 1300 AD. This part of the Americas saw the rise of several notable tribes, such as the Aztecs, the Olmecs, and the Incas (in South America). The Maya people settled in what is now central Mexico, Belize, and Guatemala. Mayan society was composed of various roles that individuals would be assigned — builders, scholars, warriors, farmers, nobles, priests, merchants, artisans — all working in harmony to grow their various cities and tribes. One's path and lot in life was determined at birth, and could usually not be changed.

The Maya had their own writing system (based on glyphs), quite similar to the ancient Egyptians. Their mastery of mathematics and astronomy was unparalleled for its time — the Mayan calendar system remains highly accurate to this day. The Maya counting system features one of the earliest uses of the number zero.

A variety of gods and deities were part of daily Maya life, most aligned to some natural element and each requiring worship and appeasement — in many cases with human sacrifice, a ritual which signified both glory and honor to the Maya selected for it. Thus many of their temples and palaces were built as places of worship.

Compared to the relative luxuries of the modern age, the life of the Maya could appear to be quite intense, savage, and extreme — but it's worth keeping in mind that this society was among the most technologically advanced on Earth for its time. The Maya were at the top of their world for almost a thousand years, and the breadth of their many accomplishments has endured over centuries.

The Mayan tribes of the Yucatán fought and defended against Spanish Conquistadors throughout the 16th century (around 1500 - 1600 AD), until eventually — after much bloodshed — the Spanish claimed victory and settled into the region for colonization.

By the year 1900, archaeologists exploring the Yucatán had discovered, studied, and photographed many of the Mayan cities in the peninsula, including Chichen Itza. The ruins of these cities were originally found reclaimed by nature and covered in lush vegetation. In time, the governments of the surrounding regions made the wise decision to restore and preserve these ancient sites for future generations to explore and learn from. Today, the Mayan cities of the Yucatán attract millions of tourists each year, just like you.

Before and After: El Castillo Pyramid (Temple of Kukulcan)

El Castillo (before restoration) photographed by Teoberto Maler, circa 1892

El Castillo as seen today (Credit: <u>santiagor12</u> - Pixabay)

TRAVEL PREPARATIONS

Hopefully the previous section has provided some insight into a few of the fascinating aspects of Mayan civilization and culture.. also note that descendants of the ancient Mayans still live and work in the Yucatán today, and many of them work in the local tourism industry to support their communities. I'm sure I don't need to convince you that the visit is worth it, so let's start planning your trip!

In this next section we'll discuss some ideas and important steps required for traveling to Mexico. With thoughtful preparation and lead time this should not be too difficult, but the factors involved will also depend on what country your passport is from.

VISAS - The Mexican government provides visa-free entry to foreign nationals of many countries, for the purposes of tourism.

As of September 2023, if you are a citizen of: the **United States**, **Canada**, the **United Kingdom** (Great Britain), **Japan, Chile, Colombia, Peru**, or any European country within the "Schengen Area" (the **indigo** or purple countries in the map below) — then all you will need is your valid, non-expired passport to enter Mexico as a tourist.

Map of the European Union "Schengen Area"

If your passport is not from one of these countries, then you will need to apply for a tourist visa to enter Mexico via the local Mexican consulate in your region. The length of this process varies per country, and could take up to 90 days (or more) in some cases.

Whether you need a visa or not, it's important to note that all foreign nationals are limited to a maximum of 180 days in Mexico.

It is possible this policy could change in the future, so it's a good idea to check the current status of your country's diplomatic / visa status with Mexico at this link — also note that the full URL will be listed in the "References" section at the end of this book.

CURRENCY - Mexico's national currency is the peso. Obtaining pesos before your trip is highly recommended, as cash is still widely used in the country — this also provides more flexibility when purchasing goods or services, since negotiating on prices with merchants is pretty common. In most banks within the United States one can order / purchase foreign currency with ease, but there is sometimes a delay if the bank needs to place a special order for a type of currency, or doesn't have the requested amount.

For example, in the US state of California (due in part to the high trade and border with Mexico) most banks either have pesos on-hand for exchange, or can obtain the requested amount within 1-2 business days. When buying any foreign currency, you will either pay a fee, or a slightly higher exchange rate than the market average — this is due to the cut the bank will make for providing the service. A good tool / app to use here is xe.com, which provides instant mid-market (average) rates for global currencies — the bank exchange rate you pay should be close, and you can always shop around.

In Mexico, prices are typically listed in pesos but they use the "$" symbol. So for a soda that you might expect to be $4 USD, you may see something like $70.00 in Mexico. This does not mean that sodas cost $70 American Dollars in Mexico — they simply use the same "dollar" symbol. Assume the prices listed are always in pesos.

Now there can be instances with dishonest merchants that will try and tell you the prices are in US dollars for whatever you're trying to buy — in this case simply walk away, or make sure this is cleared up (if possible) before you engage for a purchase. Since US dollars are widely accepted in tourist-heavy areas within Mexico, please make sure you don't fall for this more-common-than-it-should-be scam.

CREDIT CARDS - Credit cards are a reliable option and are typically safe to use — the primary reason being that credit cards offer protection against unauthorized purchases, and they don't immediately extract the cost of any purchase from your bank accounts. You have the benefit of reviewing each charge on your card before paying it. This helps immensely in case you see a charge you don't recognize — you simply call the credit card company and file a dispute for it, which is much easier than trying to recover any funds (after the fact) that were used without your knowledge.

This is what can happen with an ATM or debit card. When using a credit card you are simply much better protected, especially when traveling for any period of time abroad.

Where available, digital wallets that use "tap-to-pay" (Apple Pay, Samsung Pay, Google Pay, etc) also work very well, since these care simply another form of paying with an existing credit card — they can even mask the real credit card number with a secondary number tied only to the mobile device, as an added security layer.

FOREIGN TRANSACTION FEES - One thing to keep in mind when using credit cards is that many cards will charge a foreign transaction fee (something like 3% of the total) for any purchases made in a currency other than what the card was issued for.

However, there are credit cards that do NOT add these fees. In fact, you may already have one — and if it's not obvious, these are the cards you'll want to use the most during your trip.

In the United States, most cards issued by **Capital One** bank do not charge a fee for foreign transactions, though there are certainly others as well. Checking what fees your credit cards charge before your trip is highly advised, no matter what your budget.

Why pay these fees if you don't have to? If you'd like to review some currently available card offers, a web search for the terms "No Foreign Transaction Fee Credit Cards" can get you started.

ATM CARDS - While most established banks in Mexico use modern security technology to access global payment networks, in general you should expect a much higher degree of fraud and mechanical card interception (think credit card skimmers installed in ATM or point-of-sale machines). Be very skeptical of any terminal or ATM that is not physically on the inside of a well-known bank. Any machine with easy public access can be a target for tampering / hacking, for the purposes of stealing card information.

Personally, I do not use any kind of card while traveling that requires a PIN or physical swipe, as these methods of payment are no longer secure and both the card's magnetic stripe and your PIN can be easily compromised by a skilled actor. In general, avoid using your ATM card — even when it can be used with no PIN.

If you have no other options available, try to find a bank with an in-person teller or an ATM that is physically <u>on the inside</u> of the bank, within the lobby area. These machines are far more secure and should be safe to use. ATMs located inside of the larger resort properties are also typically safe, since security systems and resort staff keep an eye on them. You should always look for an ATM that is monitored.

Below is an example of an old-style ATM which, if located on the outside of a building or bank, is best avoided. Any **externally facing** ATM is a potential target for tampering, especially with card skimming devices that can look just like a regular ATM card reader.

Avoid unprotected ATMs like this!

I once lost around $1000 USD this way once on a foreign trip, and it took my bank over a month to investigate and recover the funds.

MOBILE PHONE USE - Before you travel, check with your mobile phone provider regarding mobile phone usage in Mexico — especially regarding roaming, network coverage, and international data use.

It is safe to assume you will use more data than you think, especially with navigation / translation apps. The major carriers in the United States will include Mexico as part of their overall network coverage for most plans, so usually no roaming charges will apply.

However if you are traveling from Europe, Canada, or other locations, using your phone in Mexico without knowing the voice / data rates can result in a massive and unexpected monthly bill.

Some plans offer daily or weekly international voice / data passes for a flat fee, which can be a good option to keep things simple. If your phone supports it, you can also look into buying a local SIM card in Mexico, but note that wireless coverage and performance may vary — and refunds for any issues around SIM cards may be a hassle.

Most areas of Mexico are covered by one of the following networks: TELCEL, Movistar, AT&T or Virgin. Usually your mobile device will auto-select an available network. You can leave this as-is, but if your phone has the option to manually select a network, enabling this may improve performance and consistency. The fastest, best-performing network in urban areas is usually **TELCEL**. Outside the cities though, set your phone to take any signal you can get.

FOOD AND WATER SAFETY - The quality and safety of water varies widely in Mexico, and a lack of precaution can sometimes lead to health issues, especially for travelers. Stories of "Montezuma's Revenge" are not entirely myths — you can get sick with nausea, vomiting, upset stomach, etc. by drinking untreated water.

In almost all urban restaurants, hotels, and resorts in Mexico you'll have the option of bottled water to purchase or provided for free. Unbottled water at fancier restaurants and resorts is also usually safe, as it's filtered on-site. Ice cubes in drinks can be a source of contamination, so unless you're in a location where the unbottled water is filtered, ask for <u>no ice</u> in your drink as a precaution. Sealed, bottled drinks (beer, soda, water) are typically safe.

In any location outside a major city or resort area, use bottled water exclusively, no exceptions.

As for food, most street vendor food you can try is typically safe, but if you're not used to the specific kind of cuisine (i.e. you try a fish or meat you're not used to) it might make sense to choose something more similar to your usual diet back home, as a precaution.

In established restaurants, the food itself will be quite safe and the issue will be more with whether you like the taste or spice level. Mexican cuisine is generally delicious and there is a wide variety or local / regional dishes to try no matter where you go.

If you know your digestion can be fussy, be sure to pack some Alka Seltzer, loperamide (anti-diarrheal), Pepto-Bismol, etc. and use the restroom <u>before</u> setting out on any long excursion. It is entirely possible to be in a (temporary) situation with no bathrooms.

ON THE SPANISH LANGUAGE - For those unaware: the official language in Mexico is Spanish. That said, it's 100% possible to visit Mexico and have an wonderful time even if you speak ***zero*** Spanish, especially if you stick to the major tourist areas and you have honest, trustworthy guides on any excursions. In addition, people who work in the travel and hospitality industry (hotels, airports, resorts, etc) will usually know some degree of functional English, at least enough to communicate with English-only travelers.

As a matter of principle though, it's better to be proactive — memorizing common tourism-related phrases and words in Spanish will make your trip much easier. As there are hundreds of English / Spanish travel guidebooks and websites available on this topic, consider this just a friendly reminder to come prepared.

Temptation Resort, Cancun

LODGING

There is no shortage of amazing places to stay in the Yucatán, and your options mostly depend on your budget and the kind of experience you'd like on your trip. Some popular location options:

1. Cancun & Hotel Zone
2. Playa Del Carmen / Mayan Riviera
3. Near Chichen Itza (inland)

Each of these has its pros and cons, but there are a number of factors to consider — ranging from budget, length of stay, amenities, access to side activities, etc. The simplest choice to start with is to decide if you want to stay at a resort or near the coast and beaches, or if you'd prefer to stay more inland at a local hotel / AirBnB, and explore the smaller towns and scenery away from the large resort areas. You could also do both, if you have the time and budget available — something I would definitely recommend.

Cancun - Hotel Zone

RESORTS - The resort properties in the Cancun area are among the best in the world, with opulent, luxurious design, fantastic amenities, and warm, inviting service. The local staff at these resorts take a lot of pride in their work, and will generally go the extra mile to make your stay an amazing one. Tips are the customary way of rewarding excellent service in Mexico, and adding a few pesos as a tip is always appreciated. Anything from 50 - 150 pesos is appropriate.

Some resort properties are also "all-inclusive", meaning for the price of your stay, most full-service meals and drinks (even alcohol) are included in the price — some properties even including room service. Let me tell you from experience this is an absolute game-changer, and a **MUST** if you want to stay near the coastline.

This type of property can be searched for on most travel sites (expedia.com, booking.com, kayak.com, etc). In addition you will generally get a concierge who can assist in transportation and information on tours, food, etc. Some resorts even offer a personal butler whose only job is to cater to your requests.

Another benefit of staying at these larger properties is that nearly everything you might want to do on a vacation (outside of actually exploring the nearby cities / attractions) is on-site. Restaurants, bars, food, swimming pools, convenience stores, souvenirs, cafeterias, nightclubs, etc. are generally within a short walking distance from your hotel room. Many of these properties feature direct beach access, but you'll often find that their on-site pools and amenities are even nicer than the actual real beaches.

Below are a few Cancun-area resort ideas to consider. You can visit their sites to get a better sense of what to expect:

1. Hotel Paradisus Playa del Carmen
2. Haven Riviera Cancun
3. Hyatt Zilara Riviera Maya

These examples are on the mid-high end of a travel budget, but are great for those willing to spend a little more to have access to numerous luxury amenities without having to leave the property. On a related note, many of the resorts in the Mayan Riviera are within 2-3 hours of the main archaeological sites on the Yucatán.

OPTIONS FURTHER INLAND - If you enjoy a more relaxed, small-town vibe when traveling, then the smaller inland cities are where you'll want to stay. The two closest to Chichen Itza are Valladolid (about 45-60 minutes away by car), or Pisté (a much smaller town, but only 10 minutes away from the ruins).

For accommodations, I suggest starting with booking.com or airbnb.com for current local rates; these sites typically offer a free cancellation window as well. Here, I'll briefly cover a few stops in the city of **Valladolid** to consider as part of any visit to the area. These landmarks are well worth a detour to experience during your trip.

Valladolid, a local coffee shop

Valladolid, San Servacio Cathedral

1) Iglesia de San Servacio

This beautiful cathedral, originally built in 1545, is situated squarely in the center of the city, as if it were the first structure built and the entire town was built around it. The building is wonderfully preserved, constructed in a traditional European style. Across the street is the central park of Valladolid; a great spot to take photos. This area is also a nice spot to rest and recharge.

Valladolid, Central Park - Francisco Cantón Rosado

Many tours from Cancun and Playa del Carmen stop in this exact area for a rest break. Usually though, the stops are quite short and there's not enough time to really explore and experience the area, so staying locally is encouraged if you like this small town vibe.

* * *

2) Caldaza de los Frailes

This is perhaps the most famous (and without question the most colorful) street in Valladolid. It is lined with decorations, merchants, cafes, restaurants, artisan shops, and all kinds of local festivities and celebrations any given week. The traditional cobblestone street and vibrant, colonial architecture gives this area a distinct old-world vibe that comes out beautifully in photos. This is certainly an area that invites a slow, leisurely walk in the morning hours with a warm cup of the local coffee — it's simply not to be missed.

Credit: Adam Jones, Ph.D. / Flickr

3) Convento de San Bernardino de Siena

This convent was completed in the mid-1500's, built by Spanish friars as a base to help spread Christianity to the Mayans who lived in the region. It's still remarkably well-preserved and functions today as a museum, featuring photos and artifacts from the era of Spanish occupation of the Yucatán. The chapel area inside is especially memorable, with an impressive rear altar wall full of religious icons.

The convent is situated at the south end of the Calzada de los Frailes, which is a lovely half-mile (0.6 km) walk from Valladolid's central park outside the Iglesia de San Servacio (#1 above). Seeing all three of these landmarks is completely possible within just two to three hours — and as an added bonus, it's great exercise!

Right outside the convent is a popular tourist photo area — you'll find a small garden path featuring large, colorful block letters spelling the city's name. If you decide to get your photo taken here, do consider that some locals may expect a small tip for doing you the favor of taking your photo with your own phone (this is the case at many tourist-filled photo spots in Mexico).

Another good option is to ask a nearby fellow tourist who is taking the same photo to take yours, you can then return the favor.

* * *

TRANSPORTATION IN MEXICO

The usual transportation options you'd expect at home are the same ones you'll have in Mexico, but the best / safest choice will vary depending on your situation (i.e. solo traveler, with a group, etc).

AIRFARE - Before any of this comes into play, you'll clearly have to arrive first. The **Cancun International Airport** (CUN) should be your initial destination, and any number of websites can help book your tickets. These websites are recommended for their search features and ease of use; they each search almost all major airlines for the best price, and offer a date/price matrix if your travel dates are flexible:

- kayak.com — my personal favorite site to book flights and car rentals; the price matrix view is an excellent tool to find the best deal for your flight dates.
- expedia.com — a good alternative to Kayak, sometimes there are deals here that Kayak doesn't show, especially when booking comprehensive vacation packages.
- orbitz.com — similar to the first two, worth checking out at least once. It has an interface similar to kayak.

The price range for flights into Mexico will vary depending on the time of year you choose to travel, and your country of origin. Seasonal demand will inflate available ticket prices, especially in the tourist-heavy summer months (May - August).

Once you arrive, you'll want to consider one of the following methods of getting around, at least for traveling long distances. From personal experience I can share some pros and cons of each below — again, the best choice is the one where you'll feel safest.

RIDESHARE / UBER - Rideshare apps typically work well in the urban areas of Mexico, where there is better wireless coverage. During the day it should be fairly easy to find a ride. The non-cash payment and ride-mapping features of these apps make them a very safe option, and recommended as a first choice if it's available.

TAXI - Taxi service is quite common in Mexico, and the availability of taxis is much better in rural areas where rideshare apps typically have little or no coverage. That said, taxis are kind of a dice roll: you can't tell the rating of the driver, how much the ride will cost upfront, or what payment methods the taxi supports.

Always assume you will need cash (in pesos) with a taxi, though some taxi services do accept credit card payments.

If you are a solo traveler, taxis are unfortunately the least safe option (especially for women). Given the negatives, consider other alternatives first before choosing to hire a taxi.

RENTAL CARS - While the process of renting a car in Mexico is about the same as anywhere else, renting a car in a foreign country involves some level of risk. Driving in Mexico can be quite disorganized and even chaotic. The odds of getting in a minor accident or inadvertently breaking a traffic law are far greater.

Then there are the added complications around insurance coverage, what happens if the vehicle is damaged, etc. I would not suggest renting a car unless you will have some kind of extended stay in the area AND you have experience as a driver in Mexico.

If you do rent, go with an established company (Avis, Hertz, Budget) — and invest in the liability insurances offered.

TOURS - Tours are a big business in Mexico, and for good reason: they provide necessary transportation to and from attractions, often with door-to-door service, for a fixed cost. The tour companies value their online reputation (as it drives sales) so they are incentivized to provide excellent service you'll want to write a good review about.

A quick search online can easily find a reputable tour to nearly any attraction in Mexico, and almost all the details are taken care of for you. While not always the cheapest option, a tour group can provide a hassle-free experience at very reasonable prices. For traveling to Chichen Itza especially, this is the suggested approach.

Here are a few of the best websites I have come across for tours. They offer easy cancellation and a wide variety of interesting tour / attraction packages at very reasonable prices.

I have been on tours from each of these companies and the experiences were excellent — everything I expected was delivered as promised, and on time. Look for tours with a lot of good reviews.

- **Viator** — A subsidiary of TripAdvisor, highly recommended as a starting point: *www.viator.com*
- **Amigo Tours** — Based in Mexico City, and winner of multiple TripAdvisor awards for their tours: *amigotours.com*
- **Cancun Adventure** — a great option for exploring the cenotes of the Yucatán: *www.cancun-adventure.com*

If you are a first-time visitor to Mexico, your 100% best choice is to book a reputable tour, since nearly everything is taken care of for you — you won't even have to know much Spanish, since at least one guide on the tour group will speak English and translate for you.

* * *

INTO THE YUCATÁN

By now I hope you've gotten the strong itch to see Chichen Itza, and that this guide has helped provide practical information about your trip, decide on a place to stay, transportation, etc.

Here we will briefly go over the final few items before you begin your journey. I am assuming now that you're already arrived in Mexico and have a place to stay, but it's not close to Chichen Itza. As discussed above, there are a number of great tour options that will pick travelers up within Cancun or along the coast.

Make sure to bring cash (in pesos) for the admission fee — as of September 2023, it's **$614 MXN** ($35 USD) for foreign visitors.

TOUR SUGGESTIONS - As of September 2023, the options below feature early-morning access tours which can get you to Chichen Itza around 8:30 am, meaning a 5:00-6:00 am departure time:

- Chichen Itza, Cenote, Lunch, Tequila & Valladolid - Expedia
- Chichen Itza, Cenote, Valladolid, Tequila & Lunch - Tripadvisor

These are just two options, but both are examples of comprehensive tours that depart in the early morning hours.

Each also includes a few other activities to help round out the excursion. You might be asking — why go in the early morning?

When you arrive right as the gates open, there are the least tourists and you can maximize that time. This allows far better photographs of the ruins, without the hordes of background people in your shots. The Yucatán sun is not at its highest, and you have several hours of comfortable exploration in the early morning when the area is still relatively cool, and there are fresh morning breezes.

Also during the early morning, most of the on-site souvenir vendors are still getting settled in for the day, and are less likely to interrupt you as you are walking around the site with their requests to buy something. You will be leaving the site just as it gets busy, and the sun's heat and the jungle humidity are approaching their peak.

I say all this from personal experience, and cannot stress this enough — plan your trip to arrive at Chichen Itza <u>early</u>.

In addition, it's much easier to explore the entire site on your own, at your own pace, tour guide or not, and leave very satisfied with the experience when you arrive just as the gates open — you simply have more choices with how you spend your time.

WHAT TO PACK!

The weather in the Yucatán can be relentless and fierce. **Take the time to leave prepared** — once you're away from your hotel or with a tour, it may not be possible to simply pause everything and go purchase something you need. Wearing shorts is advised, paired with a light t-shirt or loose top / dress, and comfortable sneakers or hiking shoes. A good sun hat or cap is also a must for the afternoons. You'll need to apply <u>plenty</u> of sunscreen to protect your skin.

Below are some other suggestions — depending on your situation and travel plans, you might not need them all:

1. **A light and sturdy backpack**
2. 2-3 bottled waters per person
3. **Biodegradable Sunscreen (SPF 50-70)**
4. A full change of clothes (just in case)
5. **Headache / Digestive medicine**
6. Insect / Mosquito Repellent
7. Pack of wipes or tissues
8. Backup cell phone charger
9. Spare USB power bank
10. **Extra cash (about 400-500 pesos)**
11. Travel-size First-Aid Kit
12. Pocket hand sanitizer

If you'll be traveling with children, remember to bring just as much to take care of yourself as you would bring for them.

The Yucatán jungle can be very uncomfortable if not prepared.

Our next stop is — I'm sure you have a good guess :)

* * *

EXPLORING CHICHEN ITZA

Congratulations on getting this far! You are about to enter one of the most mysterious and fascinating places on the entire planet.

I want to stress that for many visitors, this is a once-in-a-lifetime experience — so make the most of it <u>for you</u>, don't feel obligated to stick with your tour group, or sit and listen to a bunch of history if that's not what truly interests you here. If you'd like to have a guide, by all means do so. Explore the city on your own terms!

In the time you spend here, I hope you will sense the ancient magic still present, and feel a connection to the Mayan people of long ago. We all share a common human ancestry even with our different cultures and traditions today. For me, seeing and exploring Chichen Itza was a reminder of how connected we all are, and how amazing it is that we are even alive today to have the opportunity to learn from our past. What might be waiting here for you?

Up next is a photographic guide through the city structures, with some contextual notes on the different ruins and other small tidbits about the area. Unless otherwise noted, the following images are my own — taken on a trip to the Yucatán in 2018. They are by no means unique, but it's nice to finally publish my own work!

Feel free to reference this as you walk around, or simply close this book completely and just zen out with the energy and nature that surrounds you. This is now your time here — I encourage you to make the most of it such that you can leave Chichen Itza with no regrets.

As we discuss and walk through the major structures in Chichen Itza as shown on the list below, you'll note we'll be moving in a semi-clockwise order, starting at the Visitor Center.

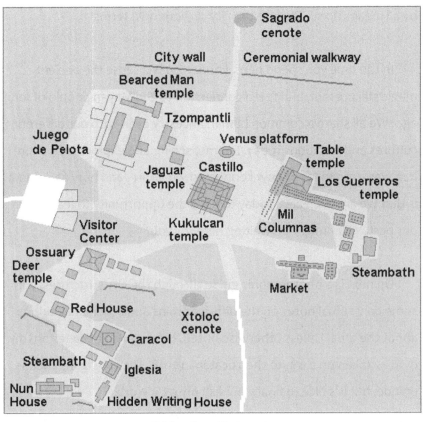

Chichen Itza - Site Layout

POINTS OF INTEREST

1. Entrance / Visitor Center
2. Temple of Kukulcan (El Castillo)
3. The Great Ball Court
4. Platform of Skulls
5. Platform of Venus
6. The Sacred Cenote
7. Temple of Warriors
8. Court of Columns
9. The Marketplace
10. Tomb of the High Priest
11. The Red House + Deer House
12. Observatory (El Caracol)
13. The House of Nuns

VISITOR CENTER AND ADMISSION FEES - You will need to purchase two tickets (in two separate lines) to access Chichen Itza: one is for the site itself, the other is a federal park (INAH) fee / tax — about **650 - 700 pesos total**, as of this writing.

IMPORTANT: Once you walk through the visitor gates, keep in mind that climbing any of the pyramids or any other structures in Chichen Itza is not permitted — this is for your own safety, and also to help preserve the delicate stone architecture.

The Temple of Kukulcan, the feathered serpent

I. The Temple of Kukulcan: "El Castillo"

Named after the Mayan feathered serpent god, this incredible pyramid sits squarely in the center of the city and was clearly of great importance; used for government and ceremonial purposes. Much has been written about it that you can read elsewhere, so I encourage you to really bask in its presence and observe its incredible construction and design. "El Castillo" means "The Castle" in Spanish — the name fits. Each side has 91 steps. The top platform is the final step, for a total of 365 steps — representing the solar year / calendar. You'll notice only two sides of the pyramid appear fully restored, with steps on the other two sides appearing worn. The temple at the top contains a ceremonial red-colored jaguar statue within. The pyramid you see is built on top of a pyramid underneath, and another underneath that one: the Mayas generally built over their existing architecture.

Credit: "A S" / Flickr

II. The Great Ball Court

Mayan warriors and athletes used this grand arena to compete in a ball game of skill and sport. Two stone goal rings stand out, positioned high on either of the side walls. There are two smaller temples that are part of the Ball Court: one at the north end known as the Temple of the Bearded Man, and another at the south entrance named the Temple of Jaguars and Shields. The sloped lower walls around the perimeter present detailed stone murals; the figures there telling an incredible story.

The victors of these games were highly revered, and ritual human sacrifice was clearly an element of the game's outcome. More than one interpretation of these murals exists — the sacrificed could have been the game's winners, or the losers, or even prisoners from other rival tribes.

Carved murals at the Ball Court

Ball Court - South Podium

The features of these Ball Court temples suggest that they served as viewing areas for spectators of the ball games, likely used by the upper class.

Ball Court - Temple of Jaguars and Shields, lower entrance

Ball Court - Temple of Jaguars and Shields, interior detail

Ball Court - Temple of the Bearded Man

III. The Platform of Skulls / Tzompantli

This structure is exactly what it's named: a platform for the display of skulls. The Mayans would place the skulls of their enemies and prisoners on wooden racks, which would then be placed on top of the platform.

This was done to intimidate rivals, and to show strength in warfare.

* * *

IV. The Platform of Venus

An elegant platform with four sides, dedicated to the planet Venus.

The detailed reliefs, stone serpent heads, and ornamentation on the sides are all very well preserved. At the right time of the year, the two entrances align to the astronomical position of Venus in the skies.

* * *

V. The Sacred Cenote / Well of Sacrifice

This natural well (locally called a "**cenote**") lies at the northern end of the city, and had a variety of uses — it was a place for religious ceremonies, ritual human sacrifice, and making offerings to the Mayan gods. The well is fairly deep: about 35 - 40 feet to the bottom. Consider that a typical swimming pool is about 6 feet deep at most for comparison. These cenotes are technically sinkholes — formed by a collapse of the limestone surface layer that exposes a cavern filled with underground water.

Archaeologists have found offerings of gold and other precious metals, as well as human remains, in the depths of this cenote.

The white gravel road ("**sacbe**") leading here from the center of the city marked the final earthly walk for those chosen to be sacrificed within.

On the near side of the cliff, the remains of a small windowed bathhouse can still be observed, along with a small platform which may have been part of some larger structure.

There's still mystery in the air here, much like a graveyard..

One final tip — it's best to stop here early in the morning of your visit, before the long path here becomes swamped with merchants selling their souvenirs and trinkets. It's easier then to get clear pictures of the area.

Sacred Cenote, alternate view / bath house

* * *

VI. The Temple of Warriors

This temple is named after the hundreds of columns which surround the vicinity — each one meticulously carved with the image of Mayan warriors. At the top of the central stairs lies a stone figure known as a "chac-mool" — this figure is often depicted in Mayan and Aztec artifacts such as pottery, small statues, or other types of artwork; it's thought to be a kind of messenger that speaks directly with the gods. The chac-mool appears as a man lying on his back, holding a small bowl where offerings can be placed.

While it's not possible to climb or enter the temple, by stepping far enough away from the front, the viewing angle changes enough to get a good glimpse of the chac-mool statue.

Detailed photos can be captured with a zoom or telephoto lens.

To the immediate left of the Temple of Warriors is another smaller pyramid, known as the Temple of the Large Tables.

Temple of the Large Tables

The design is similar to the Tomb of the High Priest, another temple which will be discussed in the next few pages. The purpose of this structure is not known with certainty, but it was likely ceremonial in nature and related in some way to the Temple of Warriors, given its close proximity.

The trees here provide a nice shade from the jungle sun.

* * *

Court of Columns, North Colonnade

VII. The Court of Columns

Next to the Temple of Warriors sits a large open area — a nearly square ring of pillars which loops around to form a large courtyard, bordered by hundreds of decorated columns. Here each distinct set of columns is unique, and is associated with a larger nearby structure.

Much like the columns at the base of the Temple of Warriors, these pillars have been intricately carved with depictions of Mayan warriors and other artifacts of battle. Around this plaza (and indeed, the entire site) you can find descriptive information plaques that provide additional historical context and details on each area you visit in the city.

In this space you will also find two other temples, one named the **Marketplace**, and another known as the **Palace of the Sculpted Columns**. Adjacent to each of these are the same numerous square and circular columns, most of them intricately carved.

This area is rich with opportunities for interesting photos, using the vast repeating columns to add perspective, vanishing points, and shadow patterns to your shots. Zooming in will reveal the unique detail of the different carvings on each individual pillar.

* * *

VIII. Tomb of the High Priest / Ossuary

Built with a similar design as El Castillo, this structure was originally a religious site; likely a place to make offerings to the various Mayan gods.

Large serpent heads adorn the base of the stairs, with detailed carvings of twisting snake bodies visible along the side facades which line the steps on each side. Consider that these carvings were crafted thousands of years ago, by hand, without any durable modern tools — yet another example of the brilliance and ingenuity of the Mayan artisans.

This temple was built on top of a subterranean cavern, where archaeologists discovered a number of tombs, likely what guided the naming of the structure as it's known today.

At one of the corners stands a large stone pillar with carvings and masks inlaid along its edges. This column was originally one of the four corners supporting what was the roof section of the temple; these columns have eroded away over time.

In front of the central staircase lies a round ceremonial platform, one of several built around the city.

Platform at the entrance to the High Priest's Tomb

IX. The Red House, The Deer House

This well-preserved structure lies a bit to the south of the Tomb of the High Priest, at the entrance to an open glade. Situated atop a tall stone platform, the building is known as the "Casa Colorada" in Spanish, due to the red coloring observed on its inside walls. Although the structure cannot be entered, the exterior shows a solid, skillful construction — especially in the fascinating detail area still visible on the roof section.

The function of this Red House is not definitely known; it may have served some civic or religious purpose, similar to other structures in the southern part of Chichen Itza. A small ball court can be found in the area directly behind the platform supporting the Red House, in what would normally be considered the "backyard"— this indicates the structure could have also been used as a residence of some kind.

Ball Court at the Casa Colorada (Red House)

A short distance away are the remains of another structure built in a similar style, known as the **Deer House**, or **Temple of the Deer**.

Not much is left here aside from its stone rubble platform and a section of the front wall, housing a pair of windows. The other walls (that have since collapsed) were said to be adorned with images of deer — this is what gives the location its name. Given its proximity to the Red House, it's a fair assumption that the Deer House was also used as a residence.

* * *

X. The Observatory: "El Caracol"

This is one the most important and unique structures in all of Mayan civilization — it's my personal favorite. Named "**El Caracol**" (meaning "the snail" in Spanish), the grounds consist of a set of elevated platforms culminating in a round structure with windows inlaid in precise, deliberate locations that align with the stars and planets (primarily Venus).

The design of the main temple indicates its use as an observatory, where Mayan astronomers could study the heavens and contribute to the greater understanding of the passage of time, the location of celestial bodies, and the Mayan calendar and numbering system.

No other structure in Chichen Itza or in any other Mayan site in the Yucatán has this same construction, signifying El Caracol's importance.

While the dome of the observatory is no longer present, it's known that there were two floors, connected by a winding stone staircase. The overall structure is built on top of an existing foundation underneath — again another key example of how the Mayans built their structures on top of one another in layers; they did not tear anything down.

El Caracol, lower front platform

This is another location which is best to visit in the early morning, as it's quite large and the morning is the easiest time to get clear, unpopulated shots. Much like at the Temple of Warriors, due to the fencing you'll need to step some distance away to alter your viewing angle, if you want to fully capture the main observatory of El Caracol in photos.

* * *

XI. The House of Nuns, The Chapel

To the south of El Caracol you'll find the last set of buildings normally accessible to the public. In this part of the city especially, you will see that the structures feature detailed, elaborate carvings on their outside walls — again providing a glimpse of the undeniable mastery of the Mayan architects and artisans who crafted them by hand centuries ago.

This complex is known as **"Las Monjas"**, named by the Spanish conquerors for the surrounding buildings' resemblance to European-style nunneries. Note the incredible craftsmanship on these walls. Pictured above is the east entrance to the **House of Nuns**, and below on the left side we have the **Chapel** (sometimes called the Church).

The Chapel, facing the north side of the House of Nuns

Given the prominent carvings of the Mayan rain god Chaac that decorate the many facades in this area, it's very likely there was some religious or ceremonial element to each of the buildings here.

Further south (set to open in late 2023) is **Chichen Viejo,** a smaller group of ruins previously accessible only to archaeologists and academics. If you get to explore this new area, please reach out and tell me what it's like!

* * *

NEARBY ATTRACTIONS

Having now discovered the wonders of Chichen Itza, you might have the urge to see more of the amazing legacy of the Mayans.

If you are staying in the Yucatán area, there are many other Mayan sites available to explore. Below are a few photos of my trip to **Tulum**, a beautiful ancient city on the coast of the Riviera Maya, about a two hour drive from Chichen Itza or Cancun.

Tulum, El Castillo (The Castle)

Tulum, Temple of the Wind God

Tulum, The House of Columns

Tulum, Viewpoint Area

A local Tulum resident enjoying the sun

Cenote X'canché, Yucatán

Another great activity to consider is to take a swim in one of the many freshwater cenotes in the region. Some cenotes feature a high dive into a refreshing swim with other tourists, while others are set up to explore the cenote's underground cave networks.

Some popular cenotes include: **Ik-Kil, X'canché, Chaak Tun, Two Eyes**, and **Sac Actún**. There are dozens of other cenotes all over the Yucatán, and each is slightly different. The ones mentioned here are highly rated on Google, and can offer a memorable experience.

SOME FINAL WORDS..

Now if you've enjoyed your time at Chichen Itza, there are many other Mesoamerican cultural sites not just in the Yucatán, but all throughout Mexico that you should consider visiting.

One of the main reasons I sought to put together this guide is to encourage others who are unfamiliar with this aspect of our shared history to give it a look — I think it's a fascinating and highly rewarding experience to share the same space and discover the way the peoples of long ago lived, if only to gain a better appreciation for how different and convenient our lives are today. So don't stop here.. there are the Mayan cities of **Coba, Uxmal,** and **Ek' Balam** — just to name a few more in the Yucatán. If you venture north near the Mexico City area, the Aztec site of **Teotihuacán** is a must-see:

Teotihuacán, Pyramid of the Sun

Teotihuacán, Pyramid of the Moon

The National Museum of Anthropology in Mexico City houses some of the most incredible artifacts discovered by archaeologists to date — a visit here is highly recommended! Pictured here are a few of my favorites.

Aztec Sun Stone — Museo Nacional de Antropología, Mexico City

Clay Animal Figurines — Museo Nacional de Antropología, Mexico City

Aztec Codex — Museo Nacional de Antropología, Mexico City

Mexico is one of the most amazing places in the world — its deep connection to early civilization, history, and culture still permeates the country today. Your visit to the Yucatán is only the beginning of your journey! I encourage you to always stay curious, and follow that urge to travel and learn about other cultures.

It's been fun writing this guide, and I do hope you have found something useful or insightful within these pages. It's incredibly rewarding for me to finally have an outlet to discuss one of my favorite topics (travel & archaeology), and also publish for the first time the photos I've taken on my past trips to Chichen Itza!

Once again, I thank you for taking the time to go through this book, and by all means if you'd like to contact me to share your feedback, a personal experience, or have any questions I can address, please reach out via email: evolutionlad@gmail.com

And finally — if you have a moment, **please consider leaving a review for this book** on the storefront where you obtained it (Amazon, iBooks, etc). This not only provides valuable feedback to others about the book, your review helps tremendously in terms of providing exposure and helping more travelers find it. Take care!

Your humble author and narrator,

-- **Andreu Limongi**

REFERENCES

~Ealasaid~. (2009, May 30). *Temptation Resort Cancun*. Flickr.

https://www.flickr.com/photos/fredrte

A S. (2017, January 21). *Ball Court, Chichen Itza*. Flickr.

https://www.flickr.com/photos/aschaf

Cartwright, M. (2023). Kukulcan. *World History Encyclopedia*.

https://www.worldhistory.org/Kukulcan

Chichen Itza. (2023). In *Wikipedia*. https://en.wikipedia.org/wiki/Chichen_Itza

Chichen Itza Ruins | Ancient buildings found at Chichen Itza. (n.d.).

https://www.chichenitza.com/ruins

Chichén Itzá The Venus Platform – Mexico Archeology. (n.d.).

https://www.mexicoarcheology.com/chichen-itza-the-venus-platform/

Dan, & Bailey. (2023, June 23). 22 things to KNOW Before visiting Chichén Itzá.

Destinationless Travel. https://destinationlesstravel.com/chichen-itza

Dearsley, B. (2021, September 13). *Visiting Chichén Itzá: 12 highlights & tips*.

PlanetWare. https://www.planetware.com/yucatan/chichen-itza-mex-yuc-ci.htm

Geggel, L. (2022, August 17). Did the Maya Really Sacrifice Their Ballgame Players?

livescience.com.

https://www.livescience.com/65611-how-to-play-maya-ballgame.html

Hake, N. (2023, June 26). Valladolid, Mexico | Ultimate Guide (+ 22 best things to do).

Travel Lemming. https://travellemming.com/valladolid-mexico

Instituto Nacional de Migración. (n.d.). *Países y regiones que requieren visa para viajar
a México*. Gobierno De México.

https://www.gob.mx/inm/documentos/paises-y-regiones-que-requieren-visa-par

a-viajar-a-mexico

Jones, A., Ph. D. (n.d.). *Global Photo Archive*. Flickr.

https://www.flickr.com/people/adam_jones

Marmor, S. (2023a, May 24). Best Sunscreen for Mexico in 2023: Biodegradable & Reef

Safe. *Travel Mexico Solo*.

https://travelmexicosolo.com/best-sunscreen-for-mexico

Marmor, S. (2023b, September 30). 10 best things to do in Valladolid Mexico in 2023.

Travel Mexico Solo.

https://travelmexicosolo.com/best-things-to-do-in-valladolid-mexico

Mellard, S. (2023, April). *Chichen Itza*. The Mayan Ruins Website.

https://www.themayanruinswebsite.com/chichen-itza.html

Mexperience. (2020, February 24). *Communications in Mexico*.

https://www.mexperience.com/mexico-essentials/communications-in-mexico

Sacred Cenote. (2023). In *Wikipedia*. https://en.wikipedia.org/wiki/Sacred_Cenote

Vázquez, S. (2022a, September 17). *Chichanchob in Chichen Itza (The Red House)*.

Mayan Peninsula. https://mayanpeninsula.com/en/chichanchob-in-chichen-itza

Vázquez, S. (2022b, September 21). *Chichen Itza - Everything you need to know for your*

trip. Mayan Peninsula. https://mayanpeninsula.com/en/chichen-itza

Cover Image: Azabache, A. (2019, November 27). Gray Pyramid on Grass Field during

Day. Pexels. https://www.pexels.com/@alexazabache/

ABOUT THE AUTHOR

Andreu is a typical American kid of the 80's: A huge fan of Lego sets, video games (especially RPG's), classic Disney animation, archaeology, Renaissance architecture, and abandoned places.

Visiting Europe and Japan are next on his bucket list.

Made in the USA
Monee, IL
28 January 2024

52550051R00039